*To Pat,*
*for whose*
*essence,*
my *love*
*is the*
*greatest*
*inspiration*
*of my life*
*and...*
*to the*
ultimate
*spiritual*
*relationship.*

# Author's Note

*Exactly* eight years ago, when I discovered THE truth about the world that sets men free, all the pain and horrible things that had been done (as well as the good ones) did not matter at all. (It was like being released from prison!) However, I saw that practically all of my friends did not and could not, at that time, share the same perspective. I found that all the things and ways of living on Earth I had questions about had to be answered *internally* because there was no one to talk to who had any answers. During the course of the next several years, I wondered about *how* I, and we, should live here in view of the fact that "life is a state of mind." This book is that realization. I wanted answers to everything from careers to our function here to sexuality to where's home. I got them. I felt like a child who finally had all his dreams end and was now ready to take his place in this dream world and rise above (while "in" it) our child-like beliefs and actions and be a *real* adult. Hence, this is a children's story *for* adults about "really" growing-up. I hope it benefits you in some tiny way. My love to you... without *you*, this would not exist.

A special thanks goes to Eden Gray... without her "commitment" to *living* absolute Truth this would never have been.

Thank you for sharing my life!

Jupiter, Florida... September 6, 1990

# Contents

# 1

# *1989 (The Alpha)*

*"But you hate to write." He said. "It's one of those tasks where you have to step aside from your ego in the controlled-consciousness world and listen and follow. And you're not a very good follower; you'd rather lead, but not at the expense of giving up your freedom. You're afraid to surrender to your inner Self and be driven. You think that your ego is something worth protecting when you 'know' it's not even your 'real' self. I AM!"*

★      ★      ★

I thought about what He had said for awhile. I knew He was right, but surrendering the control of one's human existence was something we all fight here in our dream-world called Earth.

Then the ideas and thoughts came one after another, in a barrage. It was craziness. Here I was writing on 3" x 5" note pads to capture the ideas as fast as they came.

I had never been so unstructured, so disorganized in my life. Orderliness was *the* way I kept my peace in this crazy world.

The last three months of 1989 had been an incredible time. The Eastern-block (Communist) European nations demanded and got freedom from the old tyranny of the Soviet Union... the Berlin Wall came down as well as most of the others. (Mine, too!) The number two man in the Colombian drug cartel was found and executed... not always the best solution to achieving world peace. The United States entered Panama in a surprise raid to remove a drug-connected, openly defiant military dictator who aborted his people's efforts for democratic elections by remaining in power after they voted for another.

Then, there were *my* big discoveries. I was bored with all the conventional jobs on Earth. I had tried or explored many different avenues: business for 18 years, education for one year, the military for 3 ½ years, family life and parenthood for 9 years (not including 21 years of schooling and growing up), being a free-wheeling, woman-chasing bachelor for 9 years, being a spiritual guru for 7 years (my mother used to call me "the oracle"). I'm sure I missed some things, but I have not lead a life of quiet desperation... in ego terms. However I tried and wherever I looked, I could never be satisfied.

Then I met (by choice/decision) my spiritual partner, Pat, who after bringing to my attention that "IT was happening" (meaning that the world was getting in-tune with the fact that we are all *spiritual beings* having a "human experience" and that the physical universe was nothing more than the miscreation of limitation... "Hell," in other words... by the collective-consciousness of our minds) haunted my mind gently for six weeks of my "walkabout" tour of Australia, New Zealand and Hawaii. She even had the audacity later (thank God) to tell me that she was a female version of me. (That got my attention!) In short, I could no longer deny that I didn't have the "freedom" to give love to someone that I thoroughly trusted. I was drawn to her because of her mystical mind and because she was not afraid of dying (she loved God more than any "thing").

The next difficult challenge for me is taking place right now as I write these words. I feel guided, even though my ego/humanness does not like to write *in any form*, to write this book; to give my self the freedom to listen to that Voice inside guide me to be still, and not physically active entertaining my ego as we seem to be continually doing unless we are sleeping or meditating. Yet, I recently wrote nearly two books of poetry in two days thanks to my inspiration from my relationship with Pat. So... maybe I am a writer, or... a listener, or... a *hearer*, which is more accurate. After all, if you can't "hear" the message you're listening to you can't write, speak or do anything from the heart.

Also, since I like to share my thoughts with others without a whole lot of discussion or argument, this is a very "releasing" medium of expression... provided I can be patient enough to take the time to slow my mind down to capture all these words on the page. And, it isn't easy when you're used to being active most of your life rather than sitting quietly and reading or listening.

If you don't get caught up in the idea you have to "do" something like a profession or a job to "be" someone, writing can be the most free form of function and expression on earth besides motivational speaking. There are no set hours. You do it pretty much when *you* want, *but* you do have to have a still mind in order to hear what you are being told. A lot of people may listen to the music but few may "hear" the message. You also have to free your Self from your own ego-created fear to be a writer unless you are financially well-off, or have absolutely zero material needs including hot showers and a comfortable place to sleep, not to mention food if you still need to eat. Of course, it's *all* "mind over matter" (most cliches are true... that's why they last), but you can't falter in your beliefs or you're trapped again in the limitation of Hell on Earth (which is the only place it exists).

Oh, the peace and tranquility of being focused on just *one* thing. That's the beauty of writing. You don't get scattered. You don't stay caught up in the world. You let it all go while your inner guide directs you word by word, phrase by phrase, thought by thought. Most of us are not willing to surrender being *in control* to be "possessed" by this inner guide to put down on paper everything and anything as it comes.

So, if you'll come on along, we'll take this journey together and explore the past, present and future; meet the people that come through my life; and discover the possibilities of the mind.

*       *       *

Pat looked at me and said, "You're a beautiful writer. You write from the heart."

"But, I don't know if I have anything to share with people that they would be interested in. I hate to be bored or boring. Of course, there was that time that I had that out-of-body (what I know as inner-mind) experience where I was driving down a street in Melbourne (Florida) and ended up on a parallel street a half-mile away, car and all. And, I didn't close my eyes or experience any change at all. I just *realized* that I was on the street I originally wanted to be on. 'Amazing!' I thought, and actually laughed out loud, 'how easy this mystical, beyond-the-normal stuff was… not a bit frightening.' I was elated to *know* that this really is a 'dream-world,' that we don't die since we don't exist in our bodies but in our mind (which is not the brain) and that the world could be an *interesting* place because *anything* was possible now."

"See!" she countered.

"Well, maybe you're right, Pat. Maybe I should just pick up a pen and a notepad and just start writing, but I'd rather have a lap-type computer so I could write and type at the same time. Being the efficiency expert that I've been most of my adult life, I like to do life in the simplest, most effortless way possible so that it's always fun and easy. The hell with that old Protestant work ethic that America was founded under and I was raised with where you have to work *hard* to have anything worthwhile in life. The good things in life can come fast and easy... *provided* we're not feeling unworthy because of our guilt for believing that we are separate from God (our *ultimate* fear) and that we are mere earthlings and have to *make* everything happen... such old age tripe! All it takes is for us is to be 'willing' to let it happen."

"I'm tired of working (she's a controller for a company) and all the hassles that go along with it... all the demands people make on you when you're at the top. I feel like I'm going to come into money this year (1990), and I know that things can just *come* to me," said Pat.

I agreed. We both had enough experiences on Earth to know that *anything* is possible here.

All I could say at this stage was "I think I am going to be a book writer, of God-only-knows (actually, He could care less) what form."

# Parenthetical Expression

*Life...*
*is a*
*parenthetical*
*expression*
*where I*
*learn to*
*listen to*
*this inner*
*knowingness*
*which always*
*gives me*
*this (aside)*
*information.*

# 2

# *Saturation*

"Are you sure you're just not denying yourself the opportunity to be successful in your own business?"

"Yes, Pat. I've looked at all the opportunities out there. After working for large well-known companies and small and medium sized firms in all industries from agricultural products to labor services to computer-controlled warehouses, I've had more than ample opportunity over 20 years to explore all the business possibilities; and nothing inspires me. I've pursued all things... power, fame, fortune and physical pleasure... to which we look for glory and satisfaction... and nothing "moves" me... it's all superficial... it doesn't last for more than a *moment*. And... I am tired of pursuing goals that most others go after. I want to be truly helpful to people. But, I'm finding it more appropriate now to let people live their lives the way they want without *my* direct intervention.  Having taught at the college-level and done spiritual teaching on metaphysical understanding (belief beyond the physical) very well, I feel like I've exhausted all possible areas.  There's nothing left for me to try.  I've gone from businessman to teacher to ditch-digger and back.  I've even looked into being a minister; and you've been there when I delivered a Sunday morning talk."

"Yes, and you were very loving and very good."

"Well, thanks, but that hasn't been enough.  It's just not good enough to be 'good' at something.  It has to *inspire*!  And, I guess that's what I'm trying to get across to you, Pat.  If you can't understand what I'm getting at here, I don't think there is anyone else, *I* know of, that can comprehend what happens when you reach the point of "saturation" where nothing or no one on Earth can satisfy you. Prospective business partners are concerned about profits first and have to deal with their own personal ego needs of greed stemming from poor self-esteem.  If I am going to go into business for myself I need a financial partner, so there's no way around it.  If you're going to go into business, you will need someone else's help if you're not financially independent.  Actually, business is just something for me to keep my ego busy… entertained.  It's not something I truly feel I want to do.

Money is okay, and it can make living here more convenient, which I like.  But… that's not my purpose. I came here to *bring love*, just like you.  That's our *real* 'life purpose' even if it sounds too simplistic, idealistic or impractical. I came to know or, in this case, learn *what* I am (Love... a spiritual being) and to help others understand that about themselves as well, which may not involve me opening my mouth. And, maybe that means putting my thoughts down on paper to 'share' with others.

You still have a regular job, so you haven't experienced what it's like to wander on the earth like I have for the last seven years with no 'earthly' reason for being here."

"That's true."

"Well, it's a whole different game when you get 'saturated' with *all* the things of the world and there are no more escapes. No places to run to... no people... no career... nothing! *But...* you won't leave here (physical life) until you do."

## *More and Less*

*The more*

*things you*

*want to*

*do or be*

*the* less

*you* are!

# 3

# *To Be, or Not to Be*

"My ego is almost constantly pushing me to *do* something... keep it 'entertained.' And, I've done everything under the sun it seems. I've just run out of things, and places, and people to escape to and through. It's like coming to the end of your life and saying, 'That's nice; now what? I was a pretty good human... what's next? And, please, don't send me back into the world! I have had enough suffering from believing in my limited *human-ness.*'"

Pat looked at me with those gentle, "concerned-looking" dark brown eyes of hers. It's amazing how loving "dark" eyes can be when they belong to such a gentle Spirit as her.

"It is sad but it seems that we have no self-worth here on Earth unless we 'do' something. Without a job, we have nothing to label our selves as."

"I know," she said.

"Well… I don't want to have *any* label anymore. I just want to *BE* me and accepted as nothing more than a gentle, loving spiritual being. Shakespeare had it back 300 years ago when he said, 'To be, or not to be… that is the question.' It seems like it takes us forever to wake-up… to catch on."

"That sure is true!"

"As I write these words I wonder if I have to *be* a 'writer' to write. Can't I just be a person ('persona' in Latin means 'mask') who happens to put his ideas, thoughts and feelings down on paper when he feels in-spired to do so. I'm just sharing my insides on the out-side; that's all."

"And you do it so well," Pat said sweetly. "You talk from your heart, and I love it when you come from that place."

"There has got to be another way of 'being' here on Earth where we don't focus on what people do, or look like, in order for them to have any sense of value to us. I try by just 'being' with a person and experiencing how I *feel* with them and how they seem to feel towards themselves rather than asking them what they do for a living. I could care less! We may talk about things of the world, but I am only trying (since I am learning to do this, too) to listen... to *hear* how I feel with this person... this other aspect of myself... since it is *my perception* of him that gives him all the *reality* that he has for me. In other words, *my attitude* towards people determines what they *are* for me."

Pat just continues to look lovingly at me. Silently, she sits there on the couch hardly moving a muscle. She is by far the most *intent* listener I've ever known in my life. She is the most incredible, focused audience. I've never noticed such *unconditional love* before. Such a wonderful gift to me... and such gratification for my ego... to be loved!

"Excuse me for a moment. I need to go pace... or walk... for a bit. Kind of let my body stretch and my mind clear." I stand up and stretch with my arms way up in the air. (The ego can not handle too much introspection because it knows we will realize its 'meaninglessness'... and it fears that we will let it go, which is exactly what will happen.) "Thanks. I love you."

"I love you, too, sweetheart," as she stands on her toes and gently kisses me on the lips with that innocent child-like twinkle in her eyes.

# I Have No Game... But, I'm Here

Don't ask me why I'm here
because I have no game to play.
But, I do know what I am now
after many years of attempts
to fit in and play other's games.

So, now I'll just walk on,
listen to my heart's desire
and just be me
because there truly is
nothing else to do.

# 4

# *Self-Image*

We walked along the boardwalk at the beach... an 82 degree sunny day in January (living in southern Florida along the east coast has its advantages). This is one of our favorite places to stroll and read to each other. Even though she was only 5'4" tall with a slight, curvaceous body, short red hair and a sweet innocent child-like face (which masked the fact that she was in her mid-forties), Pat always walked "tall." I thought she was 5'7" or 5'8" next to my "sleek," 6' frame when I first met her. She always projected the image of a tall person (in more ways than one). I think it was because of her bearing which always *radiated* (literally) an inner confidence and joyfulness. She always smiled at people and just... sparkled, which made them feel good about themselves.

As we walked along, I kept thinking about that *one* limiting factor in our lives that always keeps us from being what we are. Those of us who are college-educated, and therefore, more intellectual than most, tend to get caught up in our self concept of ourselves... our "self-image."

"You know what, Pat? If we didn't get caught up in our own self-*image,* life on earth would be really easy and very loving *with* everyone looking out after one another because we all *know* that we are *part* of each other. If what I see in you is my *perception* (personal interpretation) of you then all I ever see is my *image* of you. And, whatever I see in you that causes me to feel *any* discomfort is something in myself that I have some guilt about from some occurrence in my past, which in turn manifests itself as 'fear' and is then masked over by our outward expression of anger, acceptance of physical or verbal abuse, cowering or running away."

"That's true."

"Well, actually, the problem is a very simple one of getting caught up in our image of our own *ego*-self. Did you ever notice that there is a little person in every s*elf*?! That 'elf' is our ego, that 'image' that *we* created, or actually *mis*created, by merely 'believing' it to be ourselves."

"How do you stop it? How do you get rid of it?" asked Pat.

"You don't do either! You just simply stop *believing* in it... stop 'focusing' on it. Remember what my friend, Hal, said, 'This is far too important to be taken seriously.'"

She snickered a little and smiled.

The boards crunched and creaked underneath our feet as we walked purposefully with full force now as if we were walking to our destiny.

I continued, "We have gotten so caught up in our *act*, our ego, that we can't remember being anything else until something or someone like a pet, a small child or a lover touches our heart and we reach out to give them love... although our *actions* are superfluous. It's only the 'feeling' of love inside us that's important because that lovingness which commensurately creates sensations of joy and peacefulness in us extends out to *all* minds since we all are *joined* on the level of the mind (where this all takes place anyway... all this 'drama' we call *living* on Earth).

For instance, you and I have been business professionals, you in finance and me in marketing and operations management. You also have been an entertainer, so you have at least two ego self-images of your self as a 'function.' Well, what happens when something occurs and you can't *be* that thing, that function that 'doingness'?"

"I panic!"

"Right! It's just like putting these words down on paper... even though I've written three other books over the last seven years, I don't imagine ('image-in') my ego-self as a writer; therefore, I have no *identity* as one...

nor do I 'really' want one, because I've seen how hard it has been to shake my identity as a 'professional business-man' when I need to just go earn some money. The difficulty in letting go of our self-image and just being is 'tremendous'! Look how difficult it was for me recently to interview for all those professional jobs and watch them 'disappear' when I had impeccable credentials and wonderful letters of recommendation for them. I was astounded, particularly by one which asked for a back-ground in four distinctly different areas and I had expe-rience in all of them... in spades! And, they didn't hire me. I was amazed. It's very humbling. And, I guess there is no way around it... our ego... our false image of our self... our act has to be humbled until it no longer exists and only our kind, gentle, loving self... the *real* us... remains."

"That's what's happening with my job right now. I don't care about working with numbers anymore and I'm a Controller," Pat interjected.

"That's how it starts. We lose interest with our job or our partners. Instead of going inward and asking what we *really* want... to be calm and quiet... peaceful and happy... we *immediately* start looking for another *sub-stitution*... another job... another person to fill our life. We *run* from one act... one drama... to another. Almost non-stop. We seldom take time to stop and see what we are doing.

I had to be 'trashed-out' three times before I stopped. Three times I scrapped near rock-bottom before I woke up. Finally, on the third time in six years, when I lost my wonderful job, my house in the mountains and my fairy-tale princess wife, I stopped and listened. It was then that I took an inventory of my life (I had no exposure to AA-type twelve step programs at that point).

I looked at the best and the worst that I had in 38 years and was *extremely* thankful. I had two great kids that never were a problem in the seven years I helped raise them. I had the worst, nagging, over-dramatic wife and the best wife in the world. I had traveled and lived in Europe, Canada, the Caribbean and all over the United States. I had well-paid professional jobs in all sectors of business using *all* my education right from the beginning. I had lived in Manhattan, beautiful suburbs of New York, Massachusetts and Connecticut as well as skied six months of the year when I lived in Salt Lake City (my favorite place in the world). In short, I had done everything I had ever wanted to do on Earth. I had fulfilled every major dream of my life and most fantasies.

It was then that I said, 'Okay, it's all yours, Father.' And, 'Hell' *broke loose*! I had my first taste of what 'freedom' from all the trials and tribulations of earth-life feels like. I had *surrendered*!"

# Coasting

*Is there*
*any reason*
*that living*
*on Earth*
*should be* .
*a struggle?*

*Since it*
*is all*
*an illusion,*
*I think*
*I'll go*
*"coasting."*

# 5

# *Quiet Time*

After rising early in the morning, Pat would sit on the love seat in the living room, looking dainty and gentle in her navy and white striped cotton robe, with her leg crossed sophisticatedly over the other without any flesh showing except on her ankles and bare feet. She was probably the most demure lady in my life.

I sat next to her as I so often did at this time of the day, in my full-length, light-weight yellow cotton velour robe in my usual cross-legged Indian-style sitting position.

It was always soothing to sit next to her. Pat had always commented how good she felt being next to me, too. We had lost, fortunately, that dreamy-eyed romanticism that characterizes most intimate relationships between men and women... boys and girls. Instead, we have a great calm... an inner-understanding... a peaceful gentleness in each other's presence. Eye contact is seldom needed. We just need to be "next" to each other, and there's a gentle reassurance that permeates the air. The world is at peace. We are so contented... nothing else matters.

Often times we would just stare out the bay window together for the longest time. This morning we are beginning our day in the usual way watching the sun come up, twinkling through the trees.

An hour or so later, she chuckled to me, "I think you and I are going to go 'Home' (leave Earth) sitting together... on this little couch... in a booth in a restaurant... or on our favorite bright-blue, slatted wooden bench (with that great sitting angle that just cradles you) in front of the ice cream store on the beach!"

I laughed, "I can't think of a better way to go! It would amaze people how wonderful and mystical our 'quiet time' is for us... and them, too." We both agreed because we knew that the peacefulness in our minds reaches out to everyone/everything else in the universe.

## Softly

The words
come only
in the quiet
and only
"softly."

If I'm not
paying attention
they pass-on-by.

I pray
that I
will always
listen.

# 6

# *1999 (The Omega)*

*"What you believe you 'make real'... for you and for others who want to believe what you believe, too," He said. "The catch in allowing others, by sharing your ideas with them, to believe what you believe is that they want to make you a hero or an idol, someone to be looked up to for answers and guidance. And... up until this point you have not been able or, more appropriately, 'willing' to give up your 'freedom' through your anonymity. You've learned to live here on Earth in almost total obscurity and that was a good trick in view of the fact that you're a handsome man, well-educated, intelligent, personable, gregarious and charming. Your only fault was that you believed you were 'only' human for nearly 40 years. It's time to fully realize 'what' you are... as well as all your brothers... Spirit. By 1999 everyone will 'know'!"*

I had never "accepted" before *all* the things He said.

★      ★      ★

During the Summer of 1985, my friend Kathleen called one evening from Salt Lake City while I was deep in a love relationship in Melbourne, Florida which began on *July 22*. When I told her that she said, "That's a very important date because Brian (her then psychic boyfriend) said that's when the world will have attained *full* 'christhood' (meaning that everyone will realize that they are Spirit/Mind rather than a body and will live in peace and happiness forever)... on *July 22, 1999!*"

"That is great!" I said. "I know in my heart that it's true. Whatever *two* people (minds) believe can come to pass. After all, if *we* created... actually *mis*created, since it's a place of lack and limitation... the world, *NOT* God as so many believe, then we can 'see it right' by overlooking (forgiving) the anger and fear and focusing on everyone as *innocent children* playing in the sandbox.

You know, Kathleen, if enough of us begin accepting that possibility and *change our minds* about *how* we see the world then I have no doubt that we will have *total* peace and complete harmony in the physical universe by then. What a terrific possibility." I was elated because I *really* knew it was possible.

★        ★        ★

"Well, Pat, here it is nearly five years later from when I first got a glimpse of the change of humanity into a spiritual, for lack of a better word, 'body'... a oneness of *knowingness* of the 'Love' that we all are by each and every one of us.

It's like that night when we went to see the movie, *Field of Dreams,* where the man was told by a 'voice' in his mind to plow under part of his corn-field and build a baseball diamond." (And movies show us our world as it *is* currently... in thought.)

"You mean when I said, 'It's happening' when I realized that we are *all* catching on to the fact that minds communicate in various ways; people hear voices, have inner-feelings, are guided by their intuition (Spirit) like never before."

"Right!! When you said that tears began to stream down my face because I was so touched by the possibility that what Kathleen and I talked about on that summer evening on the phone was going to become a reality. And when, the ego, our belief in our *sole* reality as humans, is lifted or *released* then we usually cry. It's like being released from prison. Look at Eastern Europe in 1989. In less than 10 years from now, we are going to be freed from Hell... all of us! And, you know it too, now!

So, as each one of us realizes that our belief in our humanness has been wrong, we can make another choice of how we see ourselves and take responsibility for our *thoughts* and actions while we are still caught in this 'waking-dream' world. The *only* way out of it is to be peaceful and calm (that does not mean avoiding appropriate expression when needed in the world) in your mind at all times and let go of all *value* judging of others and the universe, to include the environment you are in at home or work."

"That's all?!"

"Yep."

"It's so simple," she said in her pert little way with that Southern accent of hers.

"I had a realization back during the Summer of 1985, and Kathleen, whom I was very joined with then on the mind-level (the only level there really is), wrote it on the back of the envelope of a letter she wrote to me approximately one month later: *Love is all there is*! When we 'feel' that; we're Home."

"That will be great."

"Thank you, Pat, for joining us."

"You're welcome. Thank you for sharing with me and sticking with me. It was tough letting go of my belief that God created the physical world and that *human* creativity was nothing (meaning not divinely inspired)."

"Well, Pat, as I've always said to you, 'You are the *doing-ness* of my 'knowingness.'" I gave her a big hug.

# Last Remaining Remnants

*It is*
*difficult*
*shedding*
*these last*
*remaining remnants*
*of my*
*humanness.*

*Earth-life*
*can be*
*a hard*
*habit*
*to break.*

# 7

# *Mystics*

Driving down the interstate south from Vero Beach (Florida) to Jupiter (about a one hour drive) during early morning is one of the most peaceful experiences for me. I get into an ethereal consciousness where I am only "half" here meaning that I'm aware of driving the car and "generally" where I am, but I am more intune with listening to the feeling of being connected with my Father (God) and the "spiritual" universe. It's like being "Home." It's very restful but hard to sustain while we are here on Earth preoccupied with all our living-life distractions and so-called "responsibilities."

It is times like this, when the warm breezes blow through the open windows of my old '75 Oldsmobile and through the pine trees and palmetto bushes lining both sides of the six-lane divided highway with hardly any traffic on it (kind of like having your own private super-highway... I love it), that I'm glad that I chose the "mystical" path Home and avoided the "psychic" route.

A lot of people involved in the metaphysical movement have overlooked the most obvious aspect of heaven on Earth... extending love and caring about others... to get engrossed in "psychic stuff" from everything from crystals to mediums and channellers (all of which work, meaning they *seem* very real on Earth, because our minds make *everything* "appear" real).

The simple distinction between a mystic and a psychic is that the mystic is only concerned with *his* or *her* "internal knowing" that the physical universe is not their ultimate reality, and they are very *aware* of their *inner-connectedness* with everyone and everything on the level of the mind where all creation (extending/ feeling love in your heart) or *mis*creation (focusing on any thing or person in the physical universe, thus making it real) takes place. The true mystic knows the mind creates it all and that our function on Earth is to realize that God did not make the physical universe; we are Spirit (a nonphysically-oriented mind, which does not truly reside in the body or the brain); life as we experience it is nothing more than a "waking" dream and no more significant or real than our "sleeping" dreams. The mystic does not ask "how" things happen.

The psychic on the other hand *focuses* on the physical universe (and therefore, adds to its continuance) and probably has the "mystical" *awareness* of the oneness of it all but forgets or overlooks the power of the mind to rise above the world. Specifically, he or she uses their "mind power" to manipulate the physical world by such activities as moving things without touching them, healing physical impairments in others or making predictions come true by merely "believing" it to be truly possible. In other words, they are better believers than most. When we reach a certain inner-knowing level in our mind, we *all* become "guided" (sometimes referred to as "psychic") to some degree to trust our *intuition/ inner-teacher* to manifest that understanding "physically" and/or verbally, such as the words on this page.

The simple difference is: the mystic is acosmic (not interested in correcting nor believing in the cosmos/ physical universe) and the psychic is cosmic (believing in the physical world and affecting changes in it through their beliefs). The psychic focuses on physical manifestation, i.e., proof and the mystic does not.

Jesus became more and more mystical as his time on earth drew to a close. That's why at the end of his ministry he told parables, so that people would find their *own* answers or connection... which is all of our responsibilities.

That's why Buddha sits smiling... the inner-knowing of the mystic!

★　　　★　　　★

When I awoke this morning and I was meditating in my beige, upholstered rocking chair, it came to me that psychics usually share openly, in a sometimes "showy" fashion, their inner knowledge of what's happening in the *universe* with the *masses*; whereas, the mystic usually keeps to himself/herself and only shares *when asked* with one or a small number of others who are *truly* interested in knowing "themselves" and are not concerned with anything but how they are in their own mind. That doesn't mean that mystics don't or won't verbalize... they just don't volunteer information unless *asked... they* tend to *ask* "questions" of others to lead them to their own *inner* recognition of the truth of "what," i.e. Spirit, they are.

Many of us go through a "psychic phase" where we go around openly sharing/talking with our friends, family and, sometimes, anyone who will listen to us about our new self-discoveries. And, this is an important aspect of our spiritual growth because we can *only* truly learn *through ourselves,* i.e., by listening to what we "say" to others, since no one can see or hear (perceive) what we do... although we can share by demonstration the *feelings* of peace and joy together, which comes from *the Love* that is us. If we don't "share," we lose the opportunity to teach *ourselves... and* that can be in any number of forms from activities to talking to writing. We came to Earth to be "physical," which, of course, is much more limited than being Mind/Spirit *(totally free)...* so, we might as well "get it out of our system" i.e., saturate, as an old lady told me in a bus station in Washington, D. C. late one evening. Then we can move on and grow to become the true "mystics" that we *all* are... and remember that we are "unconditionally loving" beings, *first!*

## *Made in the "Image"...*

*of God
is a
misnomer
because
"Thought"
as an
expression
of Love
(which is
all God is)
does not
need to
take "form."*

# 8

# *Mental Androgyny*

One morning while lying in bed with Pat I looked out at the early morning sunlight just beginning to break through the leaves rustling in the tree next to the upstairs bedroom window.  She was lying on her left side with her back to me... her usual sleeping position on the right side of the bed (creatures of habit... are we not?).

As she awoke, I said, "Hello" and gently kissed her on the lips.  "I was just lying here thinking about how our relationship has healed (gone beyond its "humanness") and progressed over the last year we've known each other.  Except for those periods where you seem to want to 'get into' your *drama* concerning work or your relationship with Jennifer (her 20 year old daughter, who was still living at home), *we* have a very mature, clear and peaceful relationship where romance and sex, which we still have, plays such a minuscule part."

"Uh-huh," she said.  "My friend, Kay, told me how

she and her husband became such good friends later in their marriage, and in their lives, when sex no longer was involved in their relationship. Their life together took on new meaning and great peace. Kay says that they are *real good* friends."

"That's great. I am glad to hear that. Although I'm *not* in favor of people practicing celibacy (or denial of any healthy practice or activity) anymore than I like any 'spiritual games' that we play, I can see that people like you and I who have had lots of sexual experiences in our lives can eventually *not care* about sex at all. In other words, we become androgynous (both male and female... non-sexual), mentally.

It seems like when we clear away the romance and sex in our boy-girl love relationships we are left with a *real* relationship where each other's *essence* (Spirit) is all that remains... and matters. Without our 'sexual' identities, we would be open to 'going-in' and becoming introspective until we found our true selves. Then we could emerge like a butterfly... gentle and innocent... into the world without our 'pretentious acts' (our egos... those *false* beliefs in our sole existence as humans/ physical beings)! Can you imagine what an incredible place this world will become when that happens? Talk about *innocence*... personified!"

Pat just looked approvingly and sweetly at me as I got into my thoughts. She seldom spoke when I went deeply into my mind... but then, that was the beauty of our relationship... the *unspoken knowingness* that exists between spiritual partners. Silence was truly "golden" for us. (If she disagrees, believe me she speaks up!)

"You know... since *we* have had several multi-orgasmic experiences together and sex to us is like going out for ice cream or any child-like craving at this point, it's no longer a big deal. It wouldn't surprise me if some day, which could be tomorrow, two weeks from now or 20 years from now, we just stopped having sex for no other reason than 'it just didn't matter any more.' I just hope that our relationship will continue forever on Earth... that we'll continue to be the spiritual partners that we were in the beginning. Imagine we *began* our relationship as it should *end... with* the *recognition* of the perfect, innocent love called 'the Christ,' which we are inside."

She kissed me gently on the lips. It was time to get up and... function.

## Beyond All Fear

*To help
take us
beyond
all forms
of fear
is
the only
purpose of
our relationship
on the
earthly-level.*

# 9

# *History of an Ordinary Mystic*

Since everything we do is for ourselves *first,* I find it appropriate to retrace my past, in general, at this point. A publisher would probably scream, "You can't do that! What about the plot... continuity?" Oh well. The mistaken assumption is that there is "order" (things follow in progression... linearly) here on Earth; but in actuality, there is none, except that which we superimpose on it. We flip back and forth to any part of our life at any point between what we think is the beginning and the end of life.

Everything, past and future, really takes place *now* since it all occurs in our mind in an *instant* (although as humans we might not be aware of it), and we just *seem* to progress very slowly from point to point and lifetime to lifetime because that's how we "like" to go. We remember the past (to include *other* ego incarnations) and envision/imagine our future... *now!* It's *always* "now." We are always living in the present. Welcome to eternity!

There is no such thing as reincarnation (living many successive lives) in reality (if there was, "Who's Jesus?"), we just "shift" *our attention* from one lifetime drama to another *just like we do in our "sleeping" dreams.* (Each of us is an "aspect" of the *one* Son of God, who is sleeping... dreaming of *us.* We are the "figures" in His dream who have taken on a life of our own. As we wake up and surrender our ego, He wakes up.) Living on Earth is no more complicated than that... we just *want* it to be, in our minds, so we can keep on dreaming. (Personally, the daytime dreams are really getting repetitious and boring.)

*     *     *

It was agreed by my parents (Howie and Bobbie... my mother hates it when I call my dad that, but he's like a childhood friend to me, now) doctors, nurses, grandparents and a whole host of other actors (not to mention my ego-self) that I arrived on the scene (literally), in the colossal movie called "Earthlife," on April 6, 1944 (that month and day is believed by the Mormons to be the *real* birth-date of Jesus, *my* most powerful spirit guide... as well as one of my spiritual teachers, Ram Dass) in Abington, Pennsylvania, just outside Philadelphia (the birthplace of American freedom).

Although my maternal grandparents lived there and I

*loved* to visit them in the summers as a young boy and play with my slightly-handicapped friend, Jacky, in the stream next to his house and my friend, Michelle, with her artistic touches in her butterfly collection and silver-smithing, I spent my elementary school years in a working-class town called Melrose, Massachusetts where you could see the outline of the city of Boston skyline about 15 miles to the southeast from the top of the hill where we lived.

When I was 12 and about to enter middle school (they used to call it junior high), my parents moved to a nicer, professional working-class town west of Greater Boston called Lexington where "The *shot* (for freedom and liberty) was heard around the world" that began the American Revolution in 1776. I finished my formal schooling there; fell into the most romantic, *Westside Story*-type relationship (without the murder at the end) with Marta, a foreign exchange student from Buenos Aires, Argentina, during our senior year of high school; and then I moved (without my family) to Wellesley, one of the wealthier yankee W.A.S.P. suburbs of Boston, to go to college.

During my last quarter of college, I met my first wife, Donna, on a blind-date. She "heard bells" according to her when I kissed her for the first time (I later told her it was the trolley car bell outside her Brookline apartment). I *bought* "her" falling-in-love-with-me story because I was extremely *needy* of having someone love me then (very co-dependent). I finished college two months later by the "skin of my teeth." We married a year later, moved to West Germany with the U. S. Army, had our first daughter, Lisa, there and returned two years later to Bridgeport, Connecticut (a real old-time working-class town), to go to graduate business school.

After finishing my last formal schooling and a two month family car trip around the entire eastern half of the United States, I got my first full-time job with a *major* corporation (who sold the subsidiary I worked for for almost "peanuts" ten months later because it was bailing out of the computer industry... I learned early, with my first job, that there was *no such thing* as "financial security," or any other kind, in the world.) My second child, Erika, came along shortly thereafter. After Donna told me almost nine years after our marriage that the *only* reason we stayed together was because we were both "cowards," I decided that "I" didn't want to be one anymore and nine months later we were divorced. I wanted "joint" custody (meaning we would alternate custodial years) because I loved my kids dearly for the seven and four years I helped raise them, respectively, and enjoyed being and playing with them both, but I did not get it. *So...* my *first* true act of "releasing/letting go" was my kids, and was by far *THE* most difficult surrender I will ever experience short of giving up my human identity in order to achieve that "relentless desire" that burns inside me for *total* freedom... to return Home. We had a *very* unhappy divorce, so I effectively lost ongoing contact with my kids which was my most difficult pain, like a living-death, for many years (I am happy to say that it is practically erased... forgiven... from my memory).

I transferred with another major corporation during the divorce process to Manhattan and began the period of ego self-development and exploration so *vital* to our human experience that until we learn to be happy with ourselves we cannot return home to that place in mind of eternal peace. After spending a year there regaining my self-confidence to live in the world as a "single" person among the "masses" and truly loving that wonderful, vibrant melting pot, I moved from the tall buildings of America's largest metropolitan city and the financial capital of the world to the high mountains of the Wasatch Mountain Range (part of the Rockies).

I spent the next fun-filled nine years in Salt Lake City (what I've always felt was the Israel of America and the only place a Jew would be considered a "gentile" meaning non-Mormon), which is the most beautiful state in the nation. I loved that wide-open, rocky desert country to wander in and to ride along the mountain-ridge road at night, feeling happy inside like a little child at Christmas time, watching all the twinkling city lights of Salt Lake, below. It was in Salt Lake, after seven years of carousing, job-hopping, skiing, physical exploration and the end of my two-month marriage and three-year relationship with my "fairy-tale princess" wife, Susan, whom I "adored," that I finally came to the understanding at age 38 that I had experienced everything and had been everywhere that I ever wanted.

In short, I felt like I had had *all* my dreams fulfilled and said, "Father, I am yours." And then, all "Hell" really *broke loose* (meaning that bit by bit my old beliefs of my role in the world and my personal desires diminished to practically nothing and I began to love... accept... myself and everyone else "as is" and for the *Love/Spirit* that we *all* are). Two years later, after much *daily* soul-searching and *much* spiritual exploration into the true meaning of life and the ultimate realization, which came to me in the *very beginning* of this period, that *God did not create the physical universe/cosmos...* that it was nothing more than the figment of our collective imagination... I left my "Nirvana."

I moved to the central, and three years later the southeast, coast of Florida where people seem to really mellow out and nature blooms all year long. Life and sunshine and light abounds in Florida! (My ego misses living on a hill and the scenic mountains and rocky desert though.) After nearly five years of living close to my parents, maternal grandmother and two daughters, I felt "at peace" in my heart with them. I have healed my unforgiveness (of their humanness) and have recognized that they did the *best* they could considering what they understand and accept.

I came to the realization that I had taken the parental rule that "children are to be seen and not heard" too personally *all* my life. That internalization was responsible for my becoming "focused" on *physical* things like female bodies, beautiful places and my own body and on my belief that "I" *personally* had no worth of any *substance* to anyone beyond my bodiliness (meaning I was *only* an "object" to be "seen"). I learned otherwise and "know" that *everyone* has value beyond their form because I can "see" (as in being "enlightened") their child-like *innocence* (sometimes referred to as the Face of Christ.) However, there remains that *shred* of humanness, that out of habit, causes me to *momentarily* forget my spiritual essence and focus on externals. But... I am very forgivable! And, now that my "life purpose" is to *bring love* (by accepting absolute truth and being at peace with everyone in the world) I am fulfilling it. See you along the road Home.

# The Game of Death

*It is
"suicide"
(which* all
*forms of
death are)
to come
to Earth
because
we only
play the
game of
death here.
(No one
comes here
to "Live.")*

# 10

# *From the Periphery*

Living in southern Florida, the land of endless summer, one gains an appreciation for the best things (particularly if you live in Palm Beach County) and the best physical environment. Walking along the soft sand at the beach two blocks from my house in Jupiter feeling "mentally" alone, I reflected on what a college professor friend of mine named Nancy, whom I used to work with, said in anger to me, "You're on the periphery of the world looking in, and no woman in the world wants anything to do with you!" She was angry that I did not play in the world by "her" rules... meaning that I did not agree with her way of seeing the world as she believed in that old Protestant work ethic that people have to work hard and have long-lasting, static careers; I would not put her ego's needs ahead of my own; plus, I did not have a steady career so that I could provide a woman with "financial security" (which I told her would *never* be my desire).

Nancy thought she was putting me down. I actually

took it as a compliment... to be considered by an "earthling" to be on the *periphery* of the world, *perceptually*. I do *not* consider myself above anyone on Earth, but her thought reminded me to not get caught up in the "games" we play here and keep my mind centered on the fact that I am a *spiritual being* (as we all are). It pleased me that Nancy saw that essence in me since she was coming from that same place in her mind in order to be able to see it in me. Hopefully soon, she will understand what it was that she was seeing in me and that was I not really a lazy individual after all, but just someone like herself who has found there is a completely different meaning to life than we have been taught all our life... that our purpose here is to express (be) the "Love" that we *are* in *whatever form* that makes us happy and brings us peace... period. We don't have to prove anything to ourselves or anyone else when we "know" *what* we are, nor do we have to play anyone else's game, i.e., accept their beliefs. I only have to acknowledge the love or the "call for love/help" (which are the *only* two things that people do) that one gives me and listen to my heart and "hear" how to respond... that's all! Could life be any simpler?

The key to learning to live *mentally* on the periphery of the world is "remembering" what you are at all times, just like an adult who remembers what he is and doesn't *act* like a child anymore. I *choose* not to act and think like *just* an earthling anymore.

## Under-the-Influence

*Have you ever...*
*been in*
*the company*
*of someone*
*"under-the-*
*influence"?*

*Well, now*
*you know*
*what it's*
*like to*
*be with*
*someone*
*who thinks*
*they are*
*only a*
*"human" being!*

# 11

# *Mind Transfer*

While we were riding down the two-lane highway through the Florida Keys on our way to Key West (the southern most point in the U.S.) through the little hamlets and over the scenic bridges spanning the turquoise green waters of the ocean, I realized that most people do not understand how the mind functions and that we are *all* joined on that level.

"Pat, you and I have experienced, as most people have without realizing it, that our minds are joined through the frequent occurrences that one of us will *begin* a sentence (usually me) and the other will *finish* it (usually you). I "think" it, and you "say" it or "do" it. People do this *all the time*, particularly, those who have lived together for awhile, such as husbands and wives, and those who have an open, heartfelt love between them as close friends do. Something (the love in them) enables them to pick up on the love (the "innocence") in another... usually with similar characteristics and learning lessons as themselves and they become drawn together.

This whole process is *mind transfer* where our thoughts and feelings move back and forth between each other as we think. Since *all* thought takes form, if only to perpetuate our existence in human (physical) form, we need to learn to "release" our thoughts by NOT *dwelling on* or *accepting* them as "real" because it is the "belief" in our thoughts that brings them to life (just like Pinocchio)... and it always takes two or more to do so (meaning that at least another person must believe in *our* power to manifest). Without another's *belief* in our thought (and they may merely pick it up telepathically and "think" that it is their own), it would not become (appear) real. If you think this isn't the truth, just look around you and remember that God would not make a physical, limited world since He's not physical Himself. *We* did, so we can never deny that we don't have any "power"... and we did it by merely *believing* in each other's thoughts! It's just that SIMPLE. (Only the human/ego mind complicates things.)

Some of us seem to have a greater affect on each other, like you and I. *Look at your hands!* When we met you had "stubs" for finger nails. Today, you have *long*, beautiful nails! I remember when we spent the weekend together this past spring (our *first* time together other than a few hours we spent at a Christmas party) I remember *thinking*, 'The *only* thing this woman is lacking is finger nails' (then my ego would be perfectly satisfied with the physical package of Pat)."

"And when you came back from your trip to Australia two months later, I had *long* finger nails for the first time in 44 years!" said Pat. "Amazing!"

"I should say so!  The thought *came to me* when I arrived back in Vero (a derivation of the Latin word, *veritas* meaning "truth") Beach that you and I had *joined* on the mind-level (heart-level) and *together* "we" had materialized your long term wish to have long nails through our *common* wish for them for you."

"Well, thank you!"

"You're welcome.  And your hands look great.  Just do me a favor and, if you ever doubt the power of our love, remember, 'LOOK AT YOUR HANDS!' And... in your own words, Pat, 'Don't be a *spiritual plebian!*'"

Pat laughed that southern belle way with a big happy smile, twinkling eyes and a deep belly laugh that always made a person feel they were really loved and appreciated. (Well... that is her *real* life purpose: "to bring love" to people by making them feel *truly* appreciated... and she does it better than anyone I know because she can really, really *listen intently* and become one with another person's drama/story *without* being affected by it. An amazing ability!)

"We all need to remember that all minds communicate; and as we grow spiritually and learn not to fear, we will become aware of this process (mind transfer) and see how we draw people into our lives."

## Original Thoughts?

*There's no
such thing
as an
"original"
thought
since
all minds
are joined.
(It just
seems "new"
to us.)*

# 12

# *Spiritual (The Real) Responsibility*

The next morning after we awoke in our motel room in Key West (a new and clean, sparkly-white, modern two-story facility) we were having pastry, juice and coffee on the second (and top) floor of the open-air (what looked like a) bell tower overlooking the blue-green water and the many inlets and small islands overgrown with mangrove. It was warm, balmy and bright. We continued our discussion of the previous day's ride down from Vero.

"You know what, Hon?" I said, while staring out over the water, to Pat who was sipping hot coffee from a styrofoam cup. "People have no idea that all their *thoughts create form* some place on Earth or in the physical universe. Every idea manifests someplace. Your thought could be materialized in some *thing*, as, some *action* or as some *new* (?) *idea in someone else's mind* clear around the other side of the globe... minds know no boundary."

Pat stared out over the water, too... but, I could tell she was listening to me, and most importantly, "hearing" what *I* was saying.

"Can you imagine how *silly* people are going to feel... and NOT guilty, I hope, because this is nothing more than a 'waking dream' that we are living (?) in... when they realize (see with *real* eyes) that they have created everything and every situation here?  Can you imagine the surprise... and the 'relief'... not to mention a little depression (self-hatred) from their *ego,* which they can choose not to listen to, when they catch on?"

"Uh-huh," she said in an under-tone.

"Actually, when universal peace and full christhood occurs by 1999, it will take place *very gently* and very slowly over the next decade.  It will probably happen so slowly that by that time people all over the world will just *BE* 'naturally' loving, helpful, generous... and trusting.  We have seen many signs that it is happening right now."

"You're right... we have... in the movies, in our families and friends and in eastern Europe."

"I guess the message we now have for our children as well as everyone is that 'YOU ARE RESPONSIBLE FOR WHATEVER YOU PUT INTO THE COLLECTIVE

CONSCIOUSNESS OF THE UNIVERSE... PLEASE BE
CAREFUL WHAT YOU THINK ABOUT OR DWELL
OR FOCUS ON!' (The life of misery we can save ourselves and each other from is our own creation.) This is
the *only* 'real' responsibility anyone has! It's our *spiritual responsibility* to ourselves, our children and everyone. So long as we only entertain loving, kind, gentle,
peaceful and happy thoughts, we will make it beyond
this life of limitation to that place *in our minds* (where
everything exists already) where we experience *total*
freedom, peace and joy."

"*We* have experienced that individually ourselves,"
said Pat, "so we *know* that there is nothing to fear by
giving up our *belief* in our humanness. Being *part* of the
'universal love' that *is* God is the greatest feeling in the
world!"

(How could I disagree with my spiritual partner?)
"Hopefully now, we are all *unlearning* our *belief* in our
humanness. That's all there is to do! *Accept* the truth
of what we all are. Could anything be simpler? Isn't
that 'understanding' and 'acceptance' the greatest *gift* we
can give to us?"

"Yes."

## Practice

*I spend
each day
learning
that life
on Earth
is my
practice
to* remember
*this is*
only
*"a movie."*

# 13

# *The New Psychology*

Psychology is the study of the mind. Since it's the "human mind" that we study, it is time that we stop "making it real" by focusing on it. In other words, the *new psychology* doesn't "study" anything (thoughts, ideas or beliefs). It is an *UN*focusing where one does not accept as credible anything or anyone, other than the expression of 'loving kindness.' All so-called sins (of the past) are merely errors in believing, and therefore focusing, on one's ego/body (humanness) as their reality.

The "new psychology" could be summarized by the following steps:

1. Accept THE truth that God did not create the world. (When we allow ourselves to let go of that belief, we will "experience" the peace and joy of being in a formless, invulnerable eternity.)

2. Expose/acknowledge to ourselves all of our fears

and egotistical attributes. (We can not build ego self-worth, which we must do *first* before going beyond it, unless we see how truly innocent we are, and therefore, totally forgivable.)

3. Keep your mind clear of negative thoughts and "dreaminess". (When they occur, we should *not guilt* ourselves about them, but instead, not *dwell* on or accept them as valid or in need of any defense or correction.)

4. Forgive/overlook "your" *perception* of others. (What you see in them is the role that *you* assigned to them through your human *projection*, which is all anyone does here.)

5. Love is all there is! So *BE* it! (We can only learn to "express" love through our *thoughts* which manifest in our "beingness" that automatically radiates from our internal feelings of loving kindness... not "needy" caretaking. This is the *only* thing we can truly learn on Earth! Everything else is superfluous.)

## Grow Up

*You have to*
*get tough*
*with yourself*
*when you get*
*caught up*
*with the world*
*and "decide"*
*to grow up*
*and stop*
*taking the*
*"dream"*
*seriously*
*and end*
*the pain.*

# 14

# It Takes One to Know One

## (No More Blame)

"When I was in an outdoor-experience program for hard-core juvenile delinquents three summers ago in western Pennsylvania, a counselor named Carol asked me before I left, 'What is the *one* thing that you would tell a child?' I looked into her gentle, *quiet*, light-blue eyes and said, 'Whatever you see in someone else is *yourself*.' (Everyone is your mirror. Your human perception comes through your attitude and value judgments of what you see in others.)"

"What did she say then?" asked Pat as we walked along South Beach in Vero.

"Nothing. Carol was very mystical. She had great internal understanding and she was only in her early 20's.

She forecast that I would leave that youth program within three months to be at peace, which was true... I lasted eight days after visiting two wilderness camps and two wagon trains. It was nice to *visit* with so many youngsters, because wherever I go (or anyone else who *knows* the truth) the Holy Spirit (the awareness of Love's presence) remains to help heal them when I'm gone... just like Jesus said. I'm not in people's lives to be a hero. Anonymity provides great freedom that psychics and faith-healers lose.

We walked along the ocean's edge for a while at a steady, slow pace without speaking a word. I enjoy our "quiet" time together. As a matter of fact, it's that kind of time that I enjoy with everyone.

"You know, Pat, if I could share one message with the universe it would be the same one I shared with Carol, only I would phrase it like the kids' cliche: 'It takes one to know one!' You can't see what you don't have *in thought*. The specific outer manifestation is not what is the same, but the *guilt/shame* we feel *inside* that creates what is on the outside.

As we know 'teaching' is when we 'call' (meaning that we are *ready* and *willing* for) certain people, unknown by us, into our lives to learn to forgive (overlook) the things we see in them that we would ordinarily *blame* them for. They are blessings in our lives, no matter how disruptive they may seem, because they are a movie screen of how we feel *inside*. If we 'react' negatively or in any way other than peacefully, then what we see in them is something we feel guilty for in the past for doing or not doing. People are reminders."

Pat chimed in, "It's such a simple thing to do... if someone arouses uncomfortable feelings in us, we need to *ask ourselves*, 'Why do I feel bad? What is it inside *me* that I feel guilt or shame for?' And then, after acknowledging it, *let it go* to be resolved by the spirit within us. Of course, we must *avoid blaming another* for his actions, which is usually our first tendency. That's a hard *habit* for most people to break! But, we must... if we are going to make it... and I know we will... soon!"

# Acknowledgment

*Only when
you look
at your
ego
completely
will you
be able
to let
it go.*

*"Acknowledgment"
is the
way it
is released.*

# 15

# *Banished from the Sandbox*

## *(Going Home)*

As I drove along the highway, on my way to who-knows-where, I pondered this unusual occurrence in my life where *all* my dreams have been fulfilled (played out), all my financial obligations have been taken care of and no one in the world is truly in *need* of my physical presence in their life. I wonder why I am still here on Earth (as my friend, Richard, would say, "Your mission is not complete yet"). It's very tough to play in someone else's "sandbox" when you don't *appreciate,* from a worldly point of view, the "game" they play. It's as if *everyone* is a "child" playing in a giant sandbox and I am sitting on the park bench watching them… particularly, since I threw away my shovel and pail seven years ago.

Romance is the biggest fantasy of all because it puts all focus *outside* our "Self" onto this boy-girl relationship drama. (This was my favorite, and last game. There are no more toys!)

I think back to about four years ago when I was riding in the car with my oldest daughter, Lisa, who was then 17 years old. She would wave to people along the way *for absolutely no reason* (she didn't know them). She is the most unconditionally loving person in my life... by whom I feel very blessed. (Probably the most inspirational... loving... point in my life was when she was born.) We have always had the highest spiritual/mystical relationship I have ever known (with my bond with Pat coming a close second)... for instance, one night while we were talking on the phone together Lisa said, "Dad, I can feel your hand holding mine." There was *always* this "unspoken understanding" between us... *real* love... "acceptance."

Looking back over the past 45 years, I've noticed, particularly in my favorite boy-girl encounters, that the "first" point of contact with another is the *highest*... that's when *perfect love* in its purest, most innocent form meets *perfect love*. After that the relationship goes "downhill" and we *focus* on ego/body stuff. If we didn't need to "play" these dramas, we could return to *freedom* (scary to those whose only reality is their body) as non-physical, eternal spirit... "Love." *Dreams* hold us back! Hold onto "one," and you keep yourself "trapped in Hell"... forever!

At this juncture in my life, I just want to live (*BE*) in a free, happy, very loving, quiet environment. I "will" that for myself... and the world... the *peace of God*. Since everything takes place in the mind first, that is where I'll find it; and from there it will manifest outwardly in my "attitude," which is the *only* thing we can correct or change in our life and the world. It's *so simple* that most of us forget repeatedly that all we have to do is "choose" how we want to see things and people in our life! The Holy Spirit (sometimes I am reminded of Him by my dad whose initials are "H.S."), my Higher Self, is my *only* friend... and He is that loving, *gentle* part in *all* minds... individually and collectively. "Individuality," preceded by our "male-/female-ness," is the *last* part of our "dream of separateness" to go! I sense my ego/humanness trying desperately to hold onto my earthly thought (thinking) process. To be ego-mindless (unfortunately attributed to senility) is the beginning step to crossing the bridge "going home."

*"Be you free!" He said.*

## Living...

*is learning
to handle
interruptions
(which are
your lessons)
without
losing your
peace of mind.*

# *Epilogue*

I came back to Salt Lake City, (the closest place to "Home" on Earth for me) where my spiritual journey began nearly eight years ago. I ran into an old friend who saw in me the reason for my coming to Earth, "You are a spiritual being. (She actually used a Hindu term meaning the same thing.) You came here not for your self, but to demonstrate the Truth for others." I then *knew* why I could never find any satisfaction from earthly goals and pleasures... the search was over! (I felt "relieved" at last.) And, I discovered that Salt Lake was no longer my home... no "place" is! But then... there is no greater freedom on Earth than where *everywhere* is your home.

*We shall*
*not cease from*
*exploration*
*and the end of all our*
*exploring*
*will be to arrive*
*where we* started
*and to know that place*
*for the first time.*

*T. S. Eliot*

*A Special Dedication...*

to my earth-father, H.S., who found his peace and kept it (appropriately) on the 4th of July, 1990... the day of freedom in America.

Thank you, Dad; I love you!

# Death...

*is the*
*transition*
*between*
*the choice*
*for "joining*
*with ALL"*
*(surrendering*
*individuality)*
*or keeping*
*(eventhough*
*formless)*
*your "awareness*
*of separateness."*